This
& INCOME
EXPENSES
LOG
BELONGS TO:

_____

_____

INCOME & EXPENSES LOG BOOK

YEAR:_____   MONTH:_____

#	DATE	DESCRIPTION	INCOME	EXPENSES	BALANCE
		TOTAL			

INCOME & EXPENSES LOG BOOK

NOTES

INCOME & EXPENSES LOG BOOK

YEAR:_____   MONTH:_____

#	DATE	DESCRIPTION	INCOME	EXPENSES	BALANCE
		TOTAL			

INCOME & EXPENSES LOG BOOK

NOTES

INCOME & EXPENSES LOG BOOK

YEAR:_____   MONTH:_____

#	DATE	DESCRIPTION	INCOME	EXPENSES	BALANCE
	TOTAL				

INCOME & EXPENSES LOG BOOK

NOTES

INCOME & EXPENSES LOG BOOK

YEAR:_____ MONTH:_____

#	DATE	DESCRIPTION	INCOME	EXPENSES	BALANCE
		TOTAL			

INCOME & EXPENSES LOG BOOK

NOTES

_____
_____
_____
_____
_____
_____
_____
_____
_____
_____
_____
_____
_____
_____
_____
_____
_____
_____
_____
_____
_____
_____
_____

INCOME & EXPENSES LOG BOOK

YEAR:_____   MONTHLY REPORT

MONTH	INCOME	EXPENSES	PROFIT
JANUARY			
FEBRUARY			
MARCH			
APRIL			
MAY			
JUNE			
JULY			
AUGUST			
SEPTEMBER			
OCTOBER			
NOVEMBER			
DECEMBER			

INCOME & EXPENSES LOG BOOK

YEAR:_____   MONTH:_____

#	DATE	DESCRIPTION	INCOME	EXPENSES	BALANCE
		TOTAL			

INCOME & EXPENSES LOG BOOK

NOTES

INCOME & EXPENSES LOG BOOK

YEAR:_____   MONTH:_____

#	DATE	DESCRIPTION	INCOME	EXPENSES	BALANCE
		TOTAL			

INCOME & EXPENSES LOG BOOK

NOTES

INCOME & EXPENSES LOG BOOK

YEAR:_____ MONTH:_____

#	DATE	DESCRIPTION	INCOME	EXPENSES	BALANCE
		TOTAL			

INCOME & EXPENSES LOG BOOK

NOTES

INCOME & EXPENSES LOG BOOK

YEAR:_____   MONTH:_____

#	DATE	DESCRIPTION	INCOME	EXPENSES	BALANCE
		TOTAL			

INCOME & EXPENSES LOG BOOK

NOTES

INCOME & EXPENSES LOG BOOK

YEAR:_____   MONTHLY REPORT

MONTH	INCOME	EXPENSES	PROFIT
JANUARY			
FEBRUARY			
MARCH			
APRIL			
MAY			
JUNE			
JULY			
AUGUST			
SEPTEMBER			
OCTOBER			
NOVEMBER			
DECEMBER			

INCOME & EXPENSES LOG BOOK

YEAR:_____   MONTH:_____

#	DATE	DESCRIPTION	INCOME	EXPENSES	BALANCE
		TOTAL			

INCOME & EXPENSES LOG BOOK

NOTES

INCOME & EXPENSES LOG BOOK

YEAR:_____ MONTH:_____

#	DATE	DESCRIPTION	INCOME	EXPENSES	BALANCE
		TOTAL			

INCOME & EXPENSES LOG BOOK

NOTES

_____

_____

_____

_____

_____

_____

_____

_____

_____

_____

_____

_____

_____

_____

_____

_____

_____

_____

_____

_____

_____

_____

_____

_____

_____

INCOME & EXPENSES LOG BOOK

YEAR:_____ MONTH:_____

#	DATE	DESCRIPTION	INCOME	EXPENSES	BALANCE
		TOTAL			

INCOME & EXPENSES LOG BOOK

NOTES

INCOME & EXPENSES LOG BOOK

YEAR:_____   MONTH:_____

#	DATE	DESCRIPTION	INCOME	EXPENSES	BALANCE
		TOTAL			

INCOME & EXPENSES LOG BOOK

NOTES

INCOME & EXPENSES LOG BOOK

YEAR:_____ MONTHLY REPORT

MONTH	INCOME	EXPENSES	PROFIT
JANUARY			
FEBRUARY			
MARCH			
APRIL			
MAY			
JUNE			
JULY			
AUGUST			
SEPTEMBER			
OCTOBER			
NOVEMBER			
DECEMBER			

INCOME & EXPENSES LOG BOOK

YEAR:_____ MONTH:_____

#	DATE	DESCRIPTION	INCOME	EXPENSES	BALANCE
		TOTAL			

INCOME & EXPENSES LOG BOOK

NOTES

INCOME & EXPENSES LOG BOOK

YEAR:_____   MONTH:_____

#	DATE	DESCRIPTION	INCOME	EXPENSES	BALANCE
		TOTAL			

INCOME & EXPENSES LOG BOOK

NOTES

INCOME & EXPENSES LOG BOOK

YEAR:_____   MONTH:_____

#	DATE	DESCRIPTION	INCOME	EXPENSES	BALANCE
		TOTAL			

INCOME & EXPENSES LOG BOOK

NOTES

INCOME & EXPENSES LOG BOOK

YEAR:_____ MONTH:_____

#	DATE	DESCRIPTION	INCOME	EXPENSES	BALANCE
	TOTAL				

INCOME & EXPENSES LOG BOOK

NOTES

INCOME & EXPENSES LOG BOOK

YEAR: _____   ## MONTHLY REPORT

MONTH	INCOME	EXPENSES	PROFIT
JANUARY			
FEBRUARY			
MARCH			
APRIL			
MAY			
JUNE			
JULY			
AUGUST			
SEPTEMBER			
OCTOBER			
NOVEMBER			
DECEMBER			

INCOME & EXPENSES LOG BOOK

YEAR:_____ MONTH:_____

#	DATE	DESCRIPTION	INCOME	EXPENSES	BALANCE
		TOTAL			

INCOME & EXPENSES LOG BOOK

NOTES

INCOME & EXPENSES LOG BOOK

YEAR:_____   MONTH:_____

#	DATE	DESCRIPTION	INCOME	EXPENSES	BALANCE
		TOTAL			

INCOME & EXPENSES LOG BOOK

NOTES

INCOME & EXPENSES LOG BOOK

YEAR:_____ MONTH:_____

#	DATE	DESCRIPTION	INCOME	EXPENSES	BALANCE
	TOTAL				

INCOME & EXPENSES LOG BOOK

NOTES

INCOME & EXPENSES LOG BOOK

YEAR:_____   MONTH:_____

#	DATE	DESCRIPTION	INCOME	EXPENSES	BALANCE
		TOTAL			

INCOME & EXPENSES LOG BOOK

NOTES

INCOME & EXPENSES LOG BOOK

YEAR:_____   MONTHLY REPORT

MONTH	INCOME	EXPENSES	PROFIT
JANUARY			
FEBRUARY			
MARCH			
APRIL			
MAY			
JUNE			
JULY			
AUGUST			
SEPTEMBER			
OCTOBER			
NOVEMBER			
DECEMBER			

INCOME & EXPENSES LOG BOOK

YEAR:_____   MONTH:_____

#	DATE	DESCRIPTION	INCOME	EXPENSES	BALANCE
		TOTAL			

INCOME & EXPENSES LOG BOOK

NOTES

INCOME & EXPENSES LOG BOOK

YEAR:_____   MONTH:_____

#	DATE	DESCRIPTION	INCOME	EXPENSES	BALANCE
		TOTAL			

INCOME & EXPENSES LOG BOOK

NOTES

INCOME & EXPENSES LOG BOOK

YEAR:_____   MONTH:_____

#	DATE	DESCRIPTION	INCOME	EXPENSES	BALANCE
	TOTAL				

INCOME & EXPENSES LOG BOOK

NOTES

INCOME & EXPENSES LOG BOOK

YEAR:_____ MONTH:_____

#	DATE	DESCRIPTION	INCOME	EXPENSES	BALANCE
		TOTAL			

INCOME & EXPENSES LOG BOOK

NOTES

INCOME & EXPENSES LOG BOOK

YEAR:_____   MONTHLY REPORT

MONTH	INCOME	EXPENSES	PROFIT
JANUARY			
FEBRUARY			
MARCH			
APRIL			
MAY			
JUNE			
JULY			
AUGUST			
SEPTEMBER			
OCTOBER			
NOVEMBER			
DECEMBER			

INCOME & EXPENSES LOG BOOK

YEAR:_____ MONTH:_____

#	DATE	DESCRIPTION	INCOME	EXPENSES	BALANCE
		TOTAL			

INCOME & EXPENSES LOG BOOK

NOTES

INCOME & EXPENSES LOG BOOK

YEAR:_____ MONTH:_____

#	DATE	DESCRIPTION	INCOME	EXPENSES	BALANCE
	TOTAL				

INCOME & EXPENSES LOG BOOK

NOTES

INCOME & EXPENSES LOG BOOK

YEAR:_____   MONTH:_____

#	DATE	DESCRIPTION	INCOME	EXPENSES	BALANCE
		TOTAL			

INCOME & EXPENSES LOG BOOK

NOTES

INCOME & EXPENSES LOG BOOK

YEAR:_____   MONTH:_____

#	DATE	DESCRIPTION	INCOME	EXPENSES	BALANCE
		TOTAL			

INCOME & EXPENSES LOG BOOK

NOTES

INCOME & EXPENSES LOG BOOK

YEAR: _____   MONTHLY REPORT

MONTH	INCOME	EXPENSES	PROFIT
JANUARY			
FEBRUARY			
MARCH			
APRIL			
MAY			
JUNE			
JULY			
AUGUST			
SEPTEMBER			
OCTOBER			
NOVEMBER			
DECEMBER			

INCOME & EXPENSES LOG BOOK

YEAR:_____   MONTH:_____

#	DATE	DESCRIPTION	INCOME	EXPENSES	BALANCE
		TOTAL			

INCOME & EXPENSES LOG BOOK

NOTES

INCOME & EXPENSES LOG BOOK

YEAR:_____   MONTH:_____

#	DATE	DESCRIPTION	INCOME	EXPENSES	BALANCE
TOTAL					

INCOME & EXPENSES LOG BOOK

NOTES

INCOME & EXPENSES LOG BOOK

YEAR:_____ MONTH:_____

#	DATE	DESCRIPTION	INCOME	EXPENSES	BALANCE
		TOTAL			

INCOME & EXPENSES LOG BOOK

NOTES

INCOME & EXPENSES LOG BOOK

YEAR:_____ MONTH:_____

#	DATE	DESCRIPTION	INCOME	EXPENSES	BALANCE
	TOTAL				

INCOME & EXPENSES LOG BOOK

NOTES

INCOME & EXPENSES LOG BOOK

YEAR:_____   MONTHLY REPORT

MONTH	INCOME	EXPENSES	PROFIT
JANUARY			
FEBRUARY			
MARCH			
APRIL			
MAY			
JUNE			
JULY			
AUGUST			
SEPTEMBER			
OCTOBER			
NOVEMBER			
DECEMBER			

INCOME & EXPENSES LOG BOOK

YEAR:_____   MONTH:_____

#	DATE	DESCRIPTION	INCOME	EXPENSES	BALANCE
		TOTAL			

INCOME & EXPENSES LOG BOOK

NOTES

INCOME & EXPENSES LOG BOOK

YEAR:_____   MONTH:_____

#	DATE	DESCRIPTION	INCOME	EXPENSES	BALANCE
		TOTAL			

INCOME & EXPENSES LOG BOOK

NOTES

INCOME & EXPENSES LOG BOOK

YEAR:_____   MONTH:_____

#	DATE	DESCRIPTION	INCOME	EXPENSES	BALANCE
		TOTAL			

INCOME & EXPENSES LOG BOOK

NOTES

INCOME & EXPENSES LOG BOOK

YEAR:_____   MONTH:_____

#	DATE	DESCRIPTION	INCOME	EXPENSES	BALANCE
		TOTAL			

INCOME & EXPENSES LOG BOOK

NOTES

INCOME & EXPENSES LOG BOOK

YEAR:_____   MONTHLY REPORT

MONTH	INCOME	EXPENSES	PROFIT
JANUARY			
FEBRUARY			
MARCH			
APRIL			
MAY			
JUNE			
JULY			
AUGUST			
SEPTEMBER			
OCTOBER			
NOVEMBER			
DECEMBER			

INCOME & EXPENSES LOG BOOK

YEAR:_____   MONTH:_____

#	DATE	DESCRIPTION	INCOME	EXPENSES	BALANCE
		TOTAL			

INCOME & EXPENSES LOG BOOK

NOTES

INCOME & EXPENSES LOG BOOK

YEAR:_____   MONTH:_____

#	DATE	DESCRIPTION	INCOME	EXPENSES	BALANCE
	TOTAL				

INCOME & EXPENSES LOG BOOK

NOTES

INCOME & EXPENSES LOG BOOK

YEAR:_____   MONTH:_____

#	DATE	DESCRIPTION	INCOME	EXPENSES	BALANCE
		TOTAL			

INCOME & EXPENSES LOG BOOK

NOTES

INCOME & EXPENSES LOG BOOK

YEAR:_____ MONTH:_____

#	DATE	DESCRIPTION	INCOME	EXPENSES	BALANCE
		TOTAL			

INCOME & EXPENSES LOG BOOK

NOTES

INCOME & EXPENSES LOG BOOK

YEAR:_____   MONTHLY REPORT

MONTH	INCOME	EXPENSES	PROFIT
JANUARY			
FEBRUARY			
MARCH			
APRIL			
MAY			
JUNE			
JULY			
AUGUST			
SEPTEMBER			
OCTOBER			
NOVEMBER			
DECEMBER			

INCOME & EXPENSES LOG BOOK

YEAR:_____   MONTH:_____

#	DATE	DESCRIPTION	INCOME	EXPENSES	BALANCE
	TOTAL				

INCOME & EXPENSES LOG BOOK

NOTES

INCOME & EXPENSES LOG BOOK

YEAR:_____   MONTH:_____

#	DATE	DESCRIPTION	INCOME	EXPENSES	BALANCE
		TOTAL			

INCOME & EXPENSES LOG BOOK

NOTES

INCOME & EXPENSES LOG BOOK

YEAR:_____   MONTH:_____

#	DATE	DESCRIPTION	INCOME	EXPENSES	BALANCE
		TOTAL			

INCOME & EXPENSES LOG BOOK

NOTES

INCOME & EXPENSES LOG BOOK

YEAR:_____   MONTH:_____

#	DATE	DESCRIPTION	INCOME	EXPENSES	BALANCE
	TOTAL				

INCOME & EXPENSES LOG BOOK

NOTES

INCOME & EXPENSES LOG BOOK

YEAR:_____   MONTHLY REPORT

MONTH	INCOME	EXPENSES	PROFIT
JANUARY			
FEBRUARY			
MARCH			
APRIL			
MAY			
JUNE			
JULY			
AUGUST			
SEPTEMBER			
OCTOBER			
NOVEMBER			
DECEMBER			

INCOME & EXPENSES LOG BOOK

YEAR:_____   MONTH:_____

#	DATE	DESCRIPTION	INCOME	EXPENSES	BALANCE
TOTAL					

INCOME & EXPENSES LOG BOOK

NOTES

INCOME & EXPENSES LOG BOOK

YEAR:_____ MONTH:_____

#	DATE	DESCRIPTION	INCOME	EXPENSES	BALANCE
TOTAL					

INCOME & EXPENSES LOG BOOK

NOTES

INCOME & EXPENSES LOG BOOK

YEAR:_____   MONTH:_____

#	DATE	DESCRIPTION	INCOME	EXPENSES	BALANCE
		TOTAL			

INCOME & EXPENSES LOG BOOK

NOTES

INCOME & EXPENSES LOG BOOK

YEAR:_____   MONTH:_____

#	DATE	DESCRIPTION	INCOME	EXPENSES	BALANCE
		TOTAL			

INCOME & EXPENSES LOG BOOK

NOTES

INCOME & EXPENSES LOG BOOK

YEAR:_____   MONTHLY REPORT

MONTH	INCOME	EXPENSES	PROFIT
JANUARY			
FEBRUARY			
MARCH			
APRIL			
MAY			
JUNE			
JULY			
AUGUST			
SEPTEMBER			
OCTOBER			
NOVEMBER			
DECEMBER			

Made in the USA
Las Vegas, NV
06 April 2021